Magicians,
Martyrs & Madmen
Tarot

Travis McHenry

Magicians,
Martyrs & Madmen
Tarot

ROCKPOOL

A Rockpool book
PO Box 252
Summer Hill NSW 2130
Australia

rockpoolpublishing.com
Follow us! **f** **⊙** rockpoolpublishing
Tag your images with #rockpoolpublishing

Originally self-published in 2022 by Travis McHenry as
Magicians, Martyrs, and Madmen Tarot

This edition published by Rockpool Publishing, 2023

ISBN: 9781922785848

Edited by Lisa Macken
Design and typesetting by Daniel Poole, Rockpool Publishing
Illustrations by Cristin Gottberg

Printed and bound in China

10 9 8 7 6 5 4 3 2 1

Contents

Minor arcana 37

Cups

Pentacles

Swords

Wands

Introduction

The *Magicians, Martyrs & Madmen Tarot* explores the depths of the human soul. Each card in the deck provides an opportunity to connect with a person from the past who can influence your present. Sometimes these people were not very nice, but even the most terrible person in the deck had one or two redeeming qualities.

I became interested in these types of characters in 1997 when I first heard the legend of Frederick Santee, a doctor who supposedly ran a coven of evil witches near my home town, and soon discovered that much that was written about these people was woefully inaccurate. To illustrate the point, virtually all information available online about Angeline Tubbs, the Witch of Saratoga, is entirely false as it was derived from a fictitious story published in 1869.

While researching and writing I sometimes became a little too attached to the magicians, martyrs and madmen and women and felt compelled to look at life through their eyes to get a better perspective on what made them so unique. Rowing an inflatable canoe across the Hudson River to camp on Esopus Island as Aleister Crowley did helped me see why it was a perfect location for his magical retreat. Travelling across every part of Romania following Vlad the Impaler from the place of his birth — now a gift shop — to the grave that held his mortal remains made it clear how challenging it must have been to rule such a vast area.

It seemed occasionally as though the connection went both ways, almost as though these souls were calling out for me to tell their story. Shortly after adding saints Sergius and Bacchus to my list of martyrs an Egyptian tour guide took me to their shrine in Cairo's Coptic Quarter. Just a few days earlier I hadn't even known these martyrs existed, but fate somehow brought me to the church holding their relics.

A few of the personalities I have chosen will touch a nerve, and some readers may question my choice of who has been included and who has been left out. While I would have loved to include everyone who was ever branded a witch, warlock, saint or serial killer, there is a limit to how much can be written. I'm devoted to telling the truth about them even when that truth diverges from the popular legend, and I have endeavoured to dig up fresh details about even the most famous of individuals. You're welcome to get outraged and hold my feet over the fire for any *opinions* I've expressed but not for stating the *facts*.

As a big, white, bald guy writing about persons of colour, I tried to be sensitive in word choices and did my best to honour cultural traditions. While reading primary sources, particularly from the 1800s, it became clear that cultural sensitivity was not always a priority for the authors. Some sources, such as records of slave transfers, were tough to read, and I discovered the horror of old financial assessments in South Carolina that listed human beings alongside furniture and livestock as mere pieces of property. These documents, along with piles of newspaper articles and out-of-print books using slurs and stereotypes of every race, from Africans to Pacific Islanders, revealed the true evils of which human beings are capable.

For those who are wondering, the idea to create a work on this subject came to me in the early 1990s when I watched *Ghostbusters II*. In that movie the ghostbusters consult the book *Magicians, Martyrs, and Madmen* while researching the fictional villain Vigo the Carpathian. Then 11 years old, I was devastated to learn that the book did not actually exist and vowed to someday bring it into reality.

How to use the cards

I n every reading you'll find there's a new lesson to be learned. As you interact with this deck and the personalities contained within you might be surprised to find you share more in common with them than you had ever imagined. Let yourself be inspired by their passion, courage and even their money-making schemes while also taking care to avoid their greed, selfishness and psychopathic tendencies.

Hopefully when you read the short biographies of these historical figures you'll discover that it doesn't take noble birth or divine favour to transform yourself into a magician, martyr or madman!

If you'd like to learn more about the people featured in this deck check out the companion book I wrote, *Magicians, Martyrs, and Madmen: A Historical Compendium*. This hefty volume was written using primary sources and includes biographical details never before published.

The pentagram spread

The pentagram spread works very well with this deck and uses five elements to create a holistic picture of any situation. You may ask a specific question to receive a rounded answer or do a general reading once a month to get a picture of what you might expect in the coming days.

- ❖ **Card 1:** overall energy of the reading
- ❖ **Card 2:** foundation
- ❖ **Card 3:** passing influences
- ❖ **Card 4:** present influences
- ❖ **Card 5:** future outcome.

The M3 spread

The symbol below and on the back of these cards is a sigil created from the 'M' glyph in the Celestial Alphabet. The glyph is repeated three times for 'Magicians', 'Martyrs' and 'Madmen', forming a sigil unique to these words that can be used for ritual work or carried as a talisman. Laying out the cards along the points of this glyph makes for an interesting reading that accesses the full potential of this deck.

- ◈ **Card 1:** existing strength
- ◈ **Card 2:** existing weakness
- ◈ **Card 3:** past mistake
- ◈ **Card 4:** present circumstances
- ◈ **Card 5:** future challenge
- ◈ **Card 6:** future accomplishment.

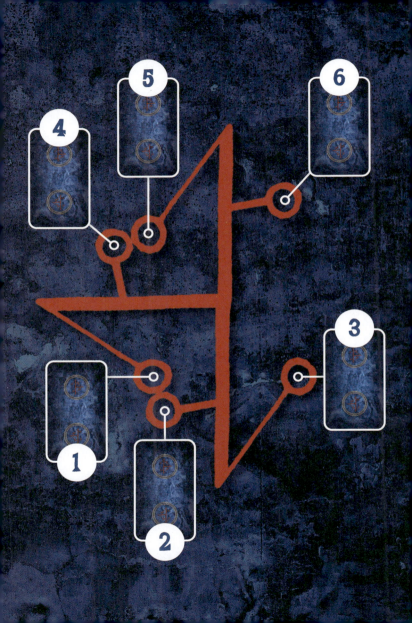

Major
arcana

0. The Fool

James Douglas

James Douglas, the 3rd Marquis of Queensberry, was considered from his youth to be an imbecile. His behaviour was so bad he had to be restrained in the basement of Holyrood Palace in Edinburgh. In 1707, at the age of nine, James escaped from his cell and murdered a cook in the kitchen. He was discovered roasting the cook's body parts over an open fire and eating pieces of the meat. The duke used his power to cover up the incident and had James locked away in an estate outside the city.

The Fool can indicate folly, mania or extravagance, although it also stands for new beginnings. As the first card in this deck James Douglas represents brash behaviour, jumping without thinking and the folly of committing acts of violence. However, it also shows a person who knows themselves, knows what they want in life and just goes for it. Sometimes we can be indecisive and wander through life without purpose or aim. James Douglas knew from the start he wanted to be a cannibal killer. He didn't wait until he was old enough to pursue his dream and he didn't wait for somebody to give him permission! He followed his instincts and listened to his heart to accomplish his goals early in life.

I. The Magician
Johann Georg Faust

Doctor Johann Faust, arguably one of the most famous magicians to have ever lived, was born in 1466 in Knittlingen, Germany. He travelled extensively throughout Europe, performing conjurations and drawing horoscopes. There is some evidence that he operated less as a ritual magician and more as a con artist. One person who had encountered him stated: 'He does not so much refer to magical arts as to tricks; and he had accomplished nothing by his idle talk and promises, being otherwise an expert in deception and imposture.'

Originally, The Magician was the mountebank or juggler, someone who entertained and perhaps even tricked their audience. The meaning has evolved into that of a ritual magician exercising control over the world around them. This card indicates the symbolic power of occult knowledge and the ability to manipulate circumstances in accordance with your will. It can represent the person for whom the reading is for if they are male.

The negative aspects of The Magician, as evidenced in the accusations of Faust being a con artist, involve trickery and possibly even outright fraud.

II. The High Priestess

Marie Laveau

Marie Laveau, the Voodoo Queen of New Orleans, was a practitioner of Haitian voodoo in Louisiana in the 1800s. Her daughter, commonly called Marie Laveau II, used her mother's name and assumed leadership of the voodoo community after her death. The elder Marie's magical practices mostly involved faith healing and the creation of charms and spells for her clients. The most common charms, called *gris gris*, were for love, money or protection against enemies.

After the local authorities banned ritual dances in Congo Square, Marie and her daughter led massive night-time voodoo rituals on a barge floating on Lake Pontchartrain. These spectacles attracted many white people who subsequently became customers of Marie Laveau.

The High Priestess is not only a companion to The Magician but is a spiritual leader in her own right. She holds the secrets of occult knowledge and shares them only with the initiated. In a reading this card can represent the person for whom the reading is for if they are female. It also stands for the divine feminine and all the authority that goes with it. Marie Laveau combined shrewd business sense with spiritual knowledge and influenced the voodoo community for generations.

III. The Empress

Elizabeth Báthory de Ecsed

THE EMPRESS III

Elizabeth Báthory de Ecsed

Countess Elizabeth Báthory was a Hungarian noblewoman who tortured and killed hundreds of young women from 1590 to 1610. Often called the 'female Dracula' or the 'Blood Countess', she was said to bathe in the blood of her victims in an effort to retain her youth and beauty. Elizabeth Báthory's crimes were less a quest for immortality and more about her enjoyment of carrying out acts of torture.

The Empress represents power over life – usually the power to create life through female fertility – although women also have the ability to take life when desired. Fertility and dominion over growth, such as the success of an agricultural crop or a business venture, can also be indicated by this card. Whatever the case, The Empress encourages the reader to seize the initiative in a matter. In a reading this card may also suggest a female love interest.

IV. The Emperor
Nero

Ruling over Rome from 54 CE until 68 CE, Nero was the last emperor from the dynasty created by Julius Caesar. His reign was troubled and he committed suicide at the age of 30. Nero murdered his mother to end her influence over him, but after her death he became a tyrant and engaged in sexual excesses with both men and women. During a Saturnalia he married one of his freed male slaves, taking the role of the bride. He was also married to a woman whom he kicked to death.

During the great fire of Rome in 64 CE Nero was said to be fiddling – playing the lute – while the city burned. This is a perfect metaphor for the decline of Rome at the hands of emperors who were more interested in gratifying their own pleasures than serving the empire as competent leaders.

The Emperor card indicates stability, power and a person of authority. It also represents an enterprise at its peak, with the possibility of decline in the future. The Emperor is usually depicted as an old man on a solid throne, but the hidden message is that all empires grow old and wither and eventually pass from the earth. Although Nero was young and Rome was still in its heyday during his reign, it did not last forever.

V. The Hierophant
Tomás de Torquemada

Tomás de Torquemada was a Dominican friar who was appointed grand inquisitor of Spain in 1483. He was known throughout Europe as the 'hammer of heretics, the light of Spain, the savior of his country, the honor of his order'. Tomás convinced the king and queen of Spain that the country was under threat from Jews and Muslims pretending to be Christians. They authorised him to arrest hundreds of heretics, who were then tortured and executed. His tribunals were so effective in their dispensation of righteous justice that Pope Alexander VI took notice and sent a team of assistant inquisitors to relieve Tomás of his authority.

Tomás was not only a grand inquisitor; he was also the personal confessor of Queen Isabella. His dual roles required him to be both a fiery denouncer of heretics and a gentle shepherd to his flock. These are the two faces of The Hierophant and the two sides present in every religion. The Hierophant represents religion, religious dogma and rigidity in beliefs. It can also indicate marriage or mercy in a reading. Any spirituality suggested by this card will have an attachment to the physical world.

VI. The Lovers (F+F)

Eva Carrière and Juliette Bisson

THE LOVERS (F+F)   VI

Eva Carrière and Juliette Bisson

Eva Carrière was an early 20th-century French medium who caused spirits to appear during séances. Juliette Bisson was her assistant, but the two women later became lovers. Before a séance Eva would usually strip naked while Juliette searched her body for any hidden material. During the performances, undertaken in a darkened room, Eva contacted guides from the spirit realm, some of whom materialised in the form of white ectoplasm.

It was later revealed that Eva's séances were hoaxes and that she had used white cheesecloth and papier-mâché to create the illusion of ghosts. One full body apparition was made using a newspaper photograph of King Ferdinand I of Bulgaria, who was still alive.

The Lovers is a card that celebrates love, beauty and companionship. This variant focuses on feminine energies and can represent two women sharing romantic feelings, a business venture between two women or even divine sisterhood. Eva could not have found success without Juliette Bisson's help. On the card the traditional angel giving a blessing is replaced by the apparition created by the women as evidence of their partnership.

VI. The Lovers (M+F)

Evita and Juan Perón

Eva Perón was an aspiring actress from a small town who in 1944 married Colonel Juan Perón, a soldier and political figure. Together they experienced a meteoric rise, eventually becoming president and first lady of Argentina.

Eva's charismatic public speeches were crucial to her husband's political fortunes. She spoke the language of the common people and endeared the Perónist regime to everyday workers, the *descamisados*. As a beautiful, assertive young woman she was idolised and admired and achieved mythic status as a folk saint to the people of Argentina, who gave her the affectionate nickname 'Evita'. However, there was also a dark side to Evita: she and her husband established sham charities and stole millions in tax revenue and union dues. They also organised the illegal detention and execution of political rivals.

The Lovers is a card that celebrates love, beauty and companionship. This variant focuses on male and female energies in harmony together. It may indicate a relationship, a business venture or romantic feelings coming from a potential lover.

VI. The Lovers (M+M)

Sergius and Bacchus

Sergius and Bacchus were two fourth-century officers in the Roman army during the reign of Emperor Diocletian. They later converted to Christianity and were martyred for refusing to enter the Temple of Jupiter in Syria. Because they had come through war and into the Christian faith together, Sergius and Bacchus felt a strong kinship with one another. Their shared feelings of affection were strong enough that they could have been considered lovers. The two soldiers underwent the ritual of *adelphopoiesis*, a kind of spiritual marriage of two men that sealed them as brothers under God.

In the 1990s Sergius and Bacchus became popular as gay saints due to their close friendship, which may or may not have been sexual, and for their spiritual bond, which could not be separated even in death.

The Lovers is a card that celebrates love, beauty and companionship. This variant focuses on male to male energy, which can take many forms: it may indicate gay sexuality, brotherhood or simply close friendship. The bond between Sergius and Bacchus might best be described as a bromance, because they stuck together as partners whether they were soldiers, teachers, Christians or martyrs.

VII. The Chariot
Pedro de Alvarado

Pedro de Alvarado was a Spanish conquistador who explored and conquered most of Central America. He often demanded tribute from indigenous peoples then brutally slaughtered them when they refused to pay.

Alvarado's entire life was devoted to warfare, and he was never satisfied with settling down to rule his various colonial possessions. Whenever he heard of a newly discovered territory that had not yet been conquered for the Spanish Crown he set off to claim it for himself, subduing the existing population with merciless brutality. Ironically, he was not killed in battle but died when his horse became spooked and trampled him to death. In the modern era it was the equivalent of a Panzer commander being run over by his own tank.

The Chariot represents war, triumph, vengeance and trouble. It can signify armed combat, but more likely it will indicate an argument or legal dispute. When reversed it nearly always means defeat. On this card Alvarado stands confidently over the body of an enemy who has been easily vanquished but he is ignorant of his horse rearing behind him, which suggests his downfall may be close at hand.

VIII. Strength
Peter Stumpp

Peter Stumpp, a successful farmer who lived near the town of Bedburg in western Germany, was responsible for murdering at least 16 men, women and children in the 1580s. From his youth he was inclined towards evil, having begun practising black magic at the age of 12. He completely rejected Christianity and embraced necromancy and sorcery, entering an incestuous relationship with his sister.

Stumpp's bloodlust grew and he began stalking and murdering any man, woman or child who caught his eye, and as the murders continued the populace began to spread rumours that a werewolf was among them. Peter, known as the Werewolf of Bedburg, was eventually captured and confessed to his crimes, and he was executed by being broken on a wheel before being chopped to pieces with an axe.

In divination the Strength card represents power, energy, action and courage. It indicates the success of a venture even though effort will still be required to achieve the final outcome. While Peter never actually turned into a werewolf as pictured on the card, his devil-summoning rituals freed him from the restraints of normal society and created a situation in which he was his authentic self: not necessarily a good thing in this circumstance!

IX. The Hermit
Edward Kelley

Edward Kelley was an Irish alchemist and ritual magician who was born in 1555 and worked closely with fellow occultist and alchemist Doctor John Dee (see card X in the major arcana). Kelley claimed to have extraordinary powers, including the ability to communicate with angels and create the philosopher's stone.

Kelley and Dee spent their first years together practising scrying, or staring into reflective surfaces in an attempt to divine the future. They also performed magic rituals to connect with angels. There is evidence they sometimes conducted séances in graveyards to connect with spirits of the dead. While travelling through Europe they gave demonstrations of their magical talents to monarchs and nobles, mostly in Germanic countries. The two magicians eventually parted ways and Kelley was arrested by Holy Roman Emperor Rudolf II for killing one of his court officials with an alchemical potion.

The Hermit embodies the alchemical traditions and the quiet solitude of an occult philosopher, but the divinatory meaning of the card is usually somewhat darker: treason, deception and corruption. The lantern carried by this figure may be used to illuminate the truth while leaving the magician obscured in shadow.

X. Wheel of Fortune
John Dee

John Dee was an alchemist and ritual magician who served in the late 1500s as court astrologer to Queen Elizabeth I. His primary forms of magic were scrying and communication with Enochian angels. As an adviser to Elizabeth I, Doctor Dee was instrumental in shaping her policies of colonisation in the New World. He also advocated for the preservation of books and the creation of a national library.

Dee's magical tools included a black mirror made of polished Aztec obsidian and a large seal of God made from pure beeswax. The seal was carved with an intricate design that allowed the magician to have direct contact with the angelic realm. On the Wheel of Fortune card this seal forms the wheel, representing an unknown fortune that may or may not appear.

The Wheel of Fortune indicates destiny, fortune and success, but it can also serve as a reminder that what goes up must come down. The original drawing of the wheel showed people in a state of flux, turned about on the wheel of life. John Dee's own life was turbulent: he was a respected professor and author who became a court favourite, only to die in poverty and obscurity.

XI. Justice

Matthew Hopkins

The man who would become the most celebrated witch finder in England, General Matthew Hopkins, was the child of a Puritan minister. After attending a witch trial he proclaimed that he had the ability to spot a witch just by looking at them.

When England collapsed into Civil War in 1642 the young Hopkins saw an opportunity to make a name for himself in the chaos that gripped the country. He and his team moved from town to town, always promising to root out witches even if the local authorities believed none were there. He quickly convinced them by producing evidence in the form of pricking, witch marks and fanciful stories about spiritual attacks against him and his associates. His book, *The Discovery of Witches*, continued to be used in the persecution of accused witches throughout Europe and in Colonial America.

The Justice card represents equality, honesty and integrity. When reversed it indicates all the negative aspects of judicial authority, including bias and the failure of a lawsuit. On the card Hopkins is depicted holding a staff and rope, which replace the traditional symbols of the Justice card with ones more applicable to a modern world in which judges are rarely blind or balanced.

XII. The Hanged Man

Gongo Lutete

THE HANGED MAN XII

Gongo Lutete

Gongo was a late 19th-century guerrilla soldier who fought during the Congo War. Raised as a slave, he won his freedom through his prowess at raiding villages and capturing slaves for his master. Once freed, Gongo became the leader of a gang of soldiers numbering in the thousands. He initially fought against the Belgian invaders but eventually joined them to fight against the Islamic slave traders.

A Belgian commander accused Gongo of being a traitor and ordered his execution. However, he wore a charmed necklace that prevented him from being killed and he survived the first salvo of bullets. A shaman revealed Gongo's secret, and they removed the necklace and fired a shot into his ear that killed him instantly.

The Hanged Man represents struggles, sacrifice and an inability to move forward. It can also indicate wisdom and the learning of secrets. On the card Gongo is depicted as being tied to a post and awaiting execution. The charmed amulet is around his neck, so he knows he cannot be killed; however, he is also aware the soldiers will eventually figure out his secret.

Gongo was stuck trying to please two factions, and in the end he angered both and ended up dead.

XIII. Death

Jack the Ripper

The most notorious serial killer of all time, Jack the Ripper had a relatively low number of victims. However, what he lacked in quantity he made up for in shear brutality. Jack murdered between five and 11 prostitutes in London's Whitechapel district from 1888 to 1891.

Each woman was savagely attacked and their bodies literally ripped to shreds, which led to speculation that the killer was a butcher or surgeon with training in anatomy. A thorough investigation yielded no solid suspects and the killings eventually stopped. The identity of Jack the Ripper remains unknown to this day.

One defining feature of the Ripper murders is his taunting of law enforcement by sending letters and writing in blood on the wall of the murder scene. His most famous letter was signed 'From Hell'.

The Death card represents endings and change leading to renewal and rebirth. Although not usually welcomed by the reader, it is not necessarily a bad card. Jack the Ripper was a product of his time: Victorian England was a sexually repressed society, and the outlet for those feelings was expressed in violent acts. The Ripper's misplaced sexual frustration foreshadowed the 20th-century's two world wars and eventual sexual liberation.

XIV. Temperance
Angeline Tubbs

Angeline Tubbs was an old woman who lived in Saratoga Springs, New York in the early 1800s. She told fortunes for a living and performed ritual magic designed to lengthen her life. Angeline, known as the Witch of Saratoga, was said to use her magic to control storms, and during the worst weather she was seen standing over the shore of Saratoga Lake laughing at the wind and waves.

One of her rituals summoned the demon Azazel, who supposedly would keep her alive so long as her cats were alive. The people of Saratoga did not regard her with animosity, and some upper class citizens became her clients. Her most popular service was horoscopes and astrological charts for young women hoping to find a husband.

The Temperance card indicates moderation, frugality and movement and can suggest a raising or lowering of the reader's fortunes. On the card Angeline is depicted controlling a storm: one hand is pointing toward the water while the other is pointing to the earth. Temperance reminds us to look in both directions before making a decision. Angeline lived a life of simplicity, earning little money and spending what she had on her cats, so this card may be a warning to more carefully govern your finances.

XV. The Devil

Delphine LaLaurie

Madame Delphine LaLaurie was born into a wealthy New Orleans family of French Creole origin. She inherited a great amount of wealth, and began torturing and killing her slaves in 1831. She mistreated all of them, whipping them relentlessly for minor offences or simply because a certain mood had come over her. Any slave who dared to disobey her was taken to the attic, where a series of small closets had been constructed for the sole purpose of restraining and torturing her victims. Delphine killed at least 12 of her slaves.

Eventually, the old cook who was chained to the stove decided she would rather die than be tortured any longer and set the house on fire. The flames brought rescuers inside, where they discovered LaLaurie's chamber of horrors in the attic.

The Devil is a card of violence, hatred, bondage, addiction and sexuality. It does not have to be evil, but it will represent a challenge. Feelings of being trapped in a situation or unable to follow your will due to repression are inherent in this card. Any sex feelings may be of a negative nature. It is possible to overcome and break binding chains, although it will take a feat of courage.

XVI. The Tower

H.H. Holmes

Herman Webster Mudgett, alias Doctor Henry Howard Holmes or H.H. Holmes, was a serial killer who murdered dozens of people, mostly women and children, from Toronto to Chicago in the mid-1800s. Holmes owned a successful drug store in Chicago and was prone to psychopathic fits of violence when faced with stressful situations beyond his control. He used loans to finance the renovation of a building with rented rooms, offices and a restaurant. The new venture couldn't repay the loans, and as Holmes underwent increasing financial pressure he began murdering the tenants to satisfy his rage. After his crimes were discovered the building became known as a murder castle.

The Tower card indicates misery, destruction and the failure of plans. It can also suggest movement, especially a change of residences. The card pictures H.H. Holmes with his building behind him. His attempt to build the castle without proper financial resources led to his downfall, similar to the hubris of building a tower to heaven only to have the almighty destroy it before you can climb to the top.

XVII. The Star

Mary I

Mary Tudor was the eldest daughter of King Henry VIII but, unlike her father, was a devout Catholic. She frequently resisted Henry's commands and reinstituted Catholicism as the state religion after his death. When she became queen in 1553 she passed the Heresy Acts, which resulted in widespread religious persecution against Protestants. Clergy who dared to continue preaching from the Church of England prayer books found themselves vanquished by flames.

During Mary's five years on the throne 300 heretics were burned at the stake. She later became a symbol for anti-Catholic sentiments in England, and her persecutions earned her the name 'Bloody Mary'.

The Star is a card of duality that symbolises love, beauty and peace, but also loss and privation. Queen Mary was an intensely spiritual woman who was kind to children, but her policies deliberately caused the deaths of hundreds of people. Behind her calm expression hangs a curtain stained with blood.

This card has a strong connection with water and movement, so whatever circumstances are present in the reader's life may be temporary.

XVIII. The Moon
Grigori Rasputin

Rasputin was born into a peasant family in central Russia in 1869. He had a religious awakening at the age of 27 and spent the rest of his life as a wandering monk and performing faith healing. His curative abilities eventually drew the attention of Tsar Nicholas II, who was in desperate search of a cure for his son's haemophilia. Rasputin performed miraculous cures for the child but also had promiscuous sex with the ladies of the imperial court. He was even accused of raping the tsar's daughter.

A group of nobles assassinated Rasputin by giving him poisoned wine, then shooting him multiple times and finally dropping him into an icy river. Soon after Nicholas abdicated from the throne, and his entire family was killed a year later. Many blamed Rasputin for his downfall.

The Moon card indicates hidden enemies, uncertainty and deception. The moon provides false light as it merely reflects the sun. Rasputin's rise to fame only came through his association with Tsar Nicholas. Connected with this falsity is deception: the truth may be obscured from your view, like Rasputin hiding the holy cross inside his tunic.

XIX. The Sun
Marquis de Sade

Donatien Alphonse François, the Marquis de Sade, was a French nobleman who was born in 1740 and lived a libertine existence. He was a prolific author, writing books that were scandalous and pornographic but at the same time scathing satires of European society. The Marquis' core philosophies were sexual liberation and the freedom to fulfil your desires. As a member of the noble class he had the resources to enact many of his fantasies, including a massive orgy with a dozen prostitutes.

His experiments with sexual bondage and pain were so shocking that his contemporaries turned his name into a new word, *sadism*, to describe anyone who finds joy in the suffering of others. Sade wasn't shy about proclaiming his love of deviant behaviour, some of which has become mainstream in the modern era.

The Sun card represents joy, happiness and the fulfilment of dreams. It is a card of victory and the manifestation of your will. Students of the traditional tarot may find it odd to see a grown man whipping a girl as the sun, but Sade's achievement of total sexual satisfaction brought him pure joy. The girl's face is not twisted in terror; she is enjoying the act as much as the man is. The sun shining through the castle window shows he's not hiding this act but doing it in the light of day.

XX. Judgement
Bender family

Operating in Kansas in the 1870s, the Benders were a family of four who murdered travellers stopping at their roadside inn. Their crimes became notorious and they were well known as the 'Bloody Benders', and the plot of land where they buried the bodies was known as 'Hell's half-acre'. The Benders were spiritualists who believed they could divine the future by communicating with the dead; they kept each body in a hole under their séance table before burying it in the orchard.

The Benders also robbed their victims, accumulating a fortune worth more than $200,000 adjusted for inflation. Twenty unfortunate travellers had their throat slit by daughter Kate, then their head bashed in by old man Bender. Mrs Bender and her son John disposed of the bodies. The Bloody Benders fled when they realised the law was on to them and their farm was excavated, which revealed the full extent of their horrible crimes.

The Judgement card indicates a change in circumstances; when it comes in a reading it should inspire ambition and progress. It can suggest a promotion or elevation of status. When the bodies were exhumed on their farm the Benders disappeared with their stolen fortune and were never heard from again, but presumably they stopped killing people and lived in relative comfort.

XXI. The World
Aleister Crowley

Aleister Crowley was an author and ritual magician who called himself the 'Beast 666'. Because of his free love philosophy, rejection of traditional religion and prolific drug use the British press named him the 'wickedest man in the world'. Originally a member of the fraternal Hermetic Order of the Golden Dawn, Crowley left and started his own religion, Thelema, in the early 1900s. It was based on inspired wisdom he obtained while in Egypt. His books blended magic ritual, astrology, the Kabbalah and occult knowledge into a single cohesive system.

Crowley eventually developed serious drug dependency that impacted his ability to lead his followers and serve as a prophet of Thelema. He influenced all ritual magicians and occultists who came after him and his philosophies were widely embraced by the counterculture movement.

The World card indicates the best of everything, along with connection with the divine and becoming one with the cosmos. This is the major arcana combined into one. Aleister Crowley's head fills the image, as though all spirituality is contained inside his physical orb. He used magic to transcend the mundane but was grounded on earth by his delight in sensual pleasures. The World is a complicated card in which the spiritual and the physical are joined.

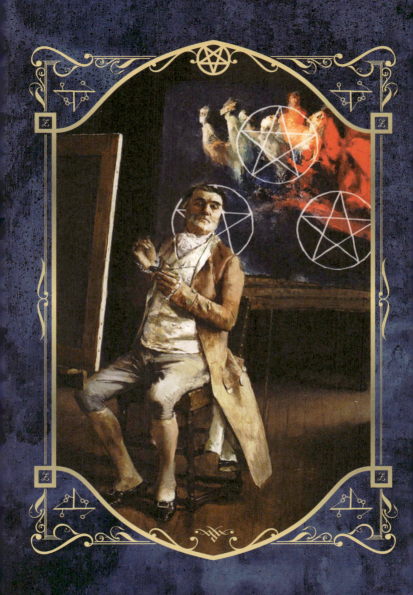

Ace of Cups
Agatha of Sicily

Agatha was a young Sicilian girl born in 231 CE during the rule of the Roman Empire. At the age of 15 she converted to Christianity and took a vow of chastity, and after her conversion she became the target of Prefect Quintianus's lustful urges although she refused to submit to his desires.

When he learned she was secretly a Christian, Quintianus subjected Agatha to many kinds of ill-treatment in an effort to get her to abandon her faith. He was compelled to throw her in prison and have her tortured; her breasts were sliced off with hot pincers. After her death she was venerated as a saint and she is the patron of rape victims, single women, nurses and breast cancer patients.

The Ace of Cups represents spirituality and good intentions that come from the heart. Saint Agatha's rise to heaven, made possible through her heartfelt devotion, allowed her to pour blessings on those who venerated her. In a reading this card indicates unexpected blessings are just around the corner.

Two of Cups
Katherina Hetzeldorfer

Katherina Hetzeldorfer holds the distinction of being one of the first women in history to be brought to trial on charges of sex with another woman. Her subsequent execution for 'crimes that cannot be named' transformed her into both a hero and martyr for the lesbian community.

Katherina fell in love with the daughter of a nobleman in Wertheim, Germany and they moved to the city of Speyer. She openly bragged to people that the girl was 'not my sister. She is my wife!' They eventually broke up and Katherina started having sex with other women in the town. When someone reported her in 1477 she was brought to trial and executed by being drowned in the Rhine River.

The Two of Cups represents love, passion and friendship. In the reversed position it can mean lust and sexual desire.

This card depicts an idyllic scene with Katherina and her lover sharing a final toast beside the Rhine River as she's drowning. As lesbian lovers in a strange town the two women depended on each other, and Katherina could not bear their separation. When her lover left she resorted to outrageous behaviour that eventually got her arrested. She preferred to be dead than to live without love.

Three of Cups

Margareta Laurentii

Margareta Laurentii lived in Kumla, Sweden and began having religious visions as a teenager in 1627. At first her visions were angelic, but they took on a sinister tone. It appeared that she was possessed by both angels and demons, which were struggling for control of her body. Once the battle was resolved Margareta began to perform miraculous healings, foretell the future and preach the gospel in public sermons.

Faithful pilgrims began to visit her, and she built up a small following. When Bishop Paulinus was sent to investigate Margareta's miracles he determined they were real, but she was also under constant spiritual attack. He returned three years later to check on her and she reported she had lost the ability to prophesy.

The Three of Cups indicates the conclusion of any matter, victory, happiness and achievement. There may be unexpected advancement. Margareta's unfortunate demonic possession turned into a blessing when a host of angels came to her defence and gave her the gift of prophecy.

Four of Cups

Franz Mesmer

Mesmer was a German physician born in 1734 who had an interest in astronomy. He developed the theory of animal magnetism and was an early pioneer of hypnosis techniques. Mesmer attempted to cure various afflictions, mostly psychological, by placing magnets against various parts of the body to move the patient's internal body fluids. His treatments seemed to work and his theories became widely popular in Europe.

Mesmer also created a form of group therapy called a *baquet*, where patients danced around a bucket full of liquid with metal rods stuck in it. An investigation into his methods determined the cures he effected were the result of his ability to influence his patients' imagination. There was no actual physical effect of his treatment; it was all in their heads.

The Four of Cups indicates ailments of the soul and problems that are not as serious as they may seem. There is a feeling of malaise present that can be impacted by the reader changing their thought patterns. On the card Mesmer's patient need only look down to the cups to effect her cure.

Five of Cups

Agnes Bernauer

From her humble beginnings as the daughter of a Bavarian barber surgeon, Agnes Bernauer eventually married the future duke of Bavaria before her tragic downfall as an accused witch. Agnes met Albert III at a jousting tournament in Augsburg in February 1428. He was immediately taken by her beauty and charm and she became his mistress, joining his household and receiving a small allowance. Due to the German laws of succession, an heir who married below his noble rank could not inherit his father's title. Albert's father arranged for Agnes to be arrested on charges of witchcraft, ostensibly for bewitching his son with a love spell. Bavarian soldiers threw her off a bridge, and she drowned in the Danube.

The Five of Cups represents family matters, including marriage. It is also a card of bitterness and frustration. Agnes began her relationship with Albert thinking she had hit the jackpot, and Albert felt the same way about Agnes. Neither realised the tragic end their marriage would have. The bridge indicates a sudden fall from grace although two cups remain upright, suggesting hope that part of the relationship and happy feelings may remain intact.

Six of Cups
Nicolas Flamel

Flamel was a French scribe and alchemist who is believed to have synthesised the philosopher's stone, granting him prolonged life and allowing him to turn lead into gold. Through his work as a manuscript dealer Flamel acquired a text of Jewish magic. When he deciphered it he discovered it contained alchemical formulas, and he spent many years conducting the experiments in the manuscript. He became one of the most successful alchemists in history. There is no record of his death, believed to be in 1418, and he was still being sighted throughout Europe 200 years after his natural life should have ended.

The Six of Cups is a card of collecting memories and remembering things from the past. Flamel is pictured on the card surrounded by the glasses and vials he used for his experiments, and he is holding the final formula for immortality. Happiness brought by remembering times past and nostalgic feelings make this card pleasant but also bittersweet, for these are things that are not in the present. Flamel's eternal life meant he would outlive all his loved ones and his success as an alchemist meant he had nothing more to learn and no more experiments to undertake, which had been his main joy in life.

Seven of Cups

Harry Houdini

Houdini was a world-renowned escape artist and magician and also a talented showman with good business sense. He enjoyed massive success with his performances, and his career was built on his elaborate escape acts. During these he would break free from straitjackets or be buried alive in coffins. These stunts were completely original and presented a form of entertainment that had never been seen before.

As a magician Houdini was the president from 1917 until his death in 1926 of the Society of American Magicians, a guild for stage magicians to work together and protect each other's interests. He died after being unexpectedly punched in the abdomen while suffering from appendicitis and performing the upside down water torture stunt. Houdini completed the stunt but died shortly after.

The Seven of Cups indicates visions of the future may not come to fruition. It is a card of ambition, although it's ambition that will not be fulfilled. Harry Houdini lived a full life and still had a very bright future ahead of him. On this card he is depicted as being suspended in a tank and he is looking outward to the cups, one of which is overflowing with money he will never get to touch.

Eight of Cups
Thomas Baker

Thomas Baker was an Australian missionary for the Methodist Church who was born in 1832. He spent nine years on the Fijian islands preaching the gospel but was murdered and eaten by a cannibal chief. Reverend Baker had the intention of doing good for the Fijian people while converting them to Christianity. He was successful as a missionary and travelled between the islands preaching and working with various clans. He learned to speak the Fijian language and respected indigenous customs.

Chief Nakatakataimoso of the Navosa tribe hated Christianity and vowed to murder any missionary who came to his village. Baker brought a small team into the chief's territory, and the following day he was murdered and eaten. He was immediately declared a martyr by the Methodists.

The Eight of Cups represents the decline of a matter and changes in home life or business. A project that has been invested in will no longer be of interest and will be abandoned. It is a card of disorder and indicates chaos on the horizon. Thomas Baker gave his life to bring the gospel to the Navosa tribe, and after killing him they eventually converted to Christianity and expressed deep remorse for having taken his life. This is thus a card of temporary decline or defeat while still holding hope for the future.

Nine of Cups
Alexander Pearce

Alexander Pearce was a convict sentenced to a brutal prison in western Tasmania. After numerous infractions and escape attempts at other prisons Pearce was deemed incorrigible and sent to the remote Macquarie Harbour penal colony. He escaped in 1822 with seven other prisoners, but they found the Tasmanian wilderness to be inhospitable and began murdering and eating one another. By the time Pearce arrived back in civilisation he was the only one left alive.

Authorities didn't believe his story of cannibalism and simply threw him back in prison. Pearce escaped again and killed his companion, and this time he was found with a human finger in his pocket. He was hung for murder shortly after.

The Nine of Cups indicates satisfaction and contentment, the realisation of your destiny and the fullness of life. Alexander Pearce is shown with nine cups of blood, enough to sate his hunger. By becoming Australia's first confirmed cannibal this otherwise unremarkable prisoner entered into legend and was studied by medical doctors, psychologists and historians.

Ten of Cups
Sawney Bean clan

The Sawney Bean clan was an incestuous family of cannibals who robbed and murdered travellers on the coast of western Scotland during the late 1500s. Sawney Bean and his wife lived in a cave, from which they robbed travellers passing through on the main road. Within two decades the clan had grown to 50 people, and they were responsible for the murdering of hundreds of people. They were finally caught and executed on orders from King James VI.

The Ten of Cups indicates the love of family and companionship. It is a card of happiness, with contentment at its heart, and can suggest enjoyment in the realm of work as well as home.

The Sawney Bean clan stuck together as a family and everyone contributed to the business of robbing, murdering and the butchering of bodies. Together they also enjoyed the rewards: feasting on meals large enough to feed a family of 50. Inside their cave authorities discovered a fortune in stolen goods, including a pile of silver and gold. The family had wealth and could have integrated with society, but they prized their freedom to live how they wished more than the creature comforts offered by the civilised world.

Page of Cups
Frederick Santee

Frederick Santee was a medical doctor who served as a homeopathic doctor and astrologer to Adolf Hitler in the late 1920s and formed a coven of witches in the small town of Wapwallopen in rural Pennsylvania. He was a child prodigy who entered Harvard at the age of 13 and graduated from Johns Hopkins medical school. While in England he was initiated into Samuel Mathers's Alpha et Omega magical fraternity (see the Page of Pentacles).

After establishing a medical practice in his tiny home town, Doctor Santee and his office staff were initiated into the New Forest wicca lineage by Sybil Leek and formed the Coven of the Catta, with Santee as the high priest. They practised ritual magic in harmony with nature and focused their devotion on cats.

The Page of Cups is a fair man who brings good news that may be connected with love or friendship, but rarely will it be reliable or permanent. This card may indicate seduction or persuasion, although of an intellectual type rather than of physical pleasures. Santee's coven celebrated ideals of beauty and knowledge and he was a generous man who often performed treatments at low cost. His friendly nature is seen on the card: sitting shirtless with a cat on his lap and enjoying the simple pleasure of wine.

Knight of Cups
Martín Ocelotl

Martín was a skilled Aztec sorcerer and businessman who predicted the arrival of the Spaniards to Montezuma II. He continued practising divination and healing during the Spanish occupation and became extremely wealthy with numerous estates of his own. He was pressured to convert to Christianity and subsequently told to stop giving prophecies, which were considered a form of heresy.

An inquisitor from Spain had him arrested and sentenced to exile in 1537, but the ship he was on disappeared at sea and he was never heard from again. It took the Inquisition over a year to find and inventory Martín's vast fortune in property, gold and other goods.

The Knight of Cups represents a proposition or an invitation. It can indicate a friend or ally, but the negative aspect of the card suggests exaggerations, lies or secrets. Martín Ocelotl was a peaceful healer who built a huge business empire from his work. His prophecies were revered by the Aztec noble class and Spanish common people alike.

QUEEN OF CUPS

La Voisin

Queen of Cups

La Voisin

The woman who would eventually gain notoriety under the name La Voisin as the deadliest poisoner in human history was born Catherine Deshayes in 1640. At the age of nine she learned the art of fortune-telling, and she gave palm readings to earn extra money for her family.

One of her most common requests as a spellcaster came from people who wanted their rich relatives to die so they could inherit their money faster. La Voisin reasoned it would be better business to sell them lethal poison, guaranteed to achieve the desired result quickly, instead of spells that were unreliable. By 1670 she was making the equivalent of $400,000 per year from her various enterprises. She was later arrested and admitted to arranging the deaths of thousands of people throughout France.

The Queen of Cups is a devoted woman who will provide good services to the reader, bringing happiness, success and pleasure. This card represents the realisation of hopes and wishes. La Voisin's criminal enterprise arose from her desire to provide a good life for her extended family. She later admitted it got out of hand due to the number of people counting on her for their livelihood, making her a perfect Queen of Cups.

King of Cups
Edward Teach

The most famous pirate to ever have lived, Edward Teach relied on psychological warfare to compel ship captains to give up their cargo without the need to resort to violence. His large black beard, adorned with burning fuses and leading to the well-known name of Blackbeard, made Teach look like a barbaric killer when he was actually an enterprising privateer always on the hunt for plunder. He was pardoned by King George I of Great Britain but found the peaceful life boring and returned to the high seas.

During the last months of 1718 Blackbeard sailed the coast of North America, robbing vessels from England. His reign of terror was put to an end during a fierce battle off the coast of Ocracoke Island, North Carolina. Teach's head was cut off and displayed on a pole over Chesapeake Bay as a warning to other pirates.

The King of Cups is a fair man involved in business, law or religion. He is responsible, and his intellect takes form in creativity. This card suggests the presence of inspiration and promotion. Blackbeard was a man of action who thrived only while he was working. His creative approach of spreading rumours that he was a violent killer helped him earn money quickly without the need to murder innocent people.

Ace of Pentacles

Lavinia Fisher

Lavinia Fisher and her husband John ran a roadside inn and tavern called the Six Mile House. They robbed and sometimes murdered travellers coming to and from the city of Charleston, South Carolina. In 1819 an angry group of citizens marched to their house and threatened to burn it down if they didn't come out. The Fishers and their gang of 10 people fled into the night but returned the following day and retook possession of the house. The sheriff arrived with a posse, arrested the entire gang and charged them with highway robbery, which was punishable by death in those days. At the public hanging John Fisher quietly accepted his fate, but Lavinia screamed, 'If you have a message for the devil, tell me now, for I shall be seeing him shortly!'

The Ace of Pentacles represents perfect contentment, ecstasy and money. Any matters currently weighing on the mind of the reader will be resolved in a satisfactory fashion, resulting in victory and success. Lavinia Fisher literally had money raining in, both from the legitimate business of Six Mile House and the criminal acts she and her husband were committing.

Two of Pentacles
Ann O'Delia Diss Debar

TWO OF PENTACLES

Ann O'Delia Diss Debar

Ann Debar, born c. 1849, was a compulsive liar who told wild stories about being the illegitimate child of King Ludwig of Bavaria. She seduced men to get money, and at one point was diagnosed as being insane. She discovered the spiritualist movement, and like other fraudsters before her she realised she could profit from exploiting families grieving their dead loved ones. Harry Houdini investigated her claims and declared her to be the 'most extraordinary fake medium the world has ever known'. Ann was eventually arrested for fraud and moved to London, calling herself Swami Lara Horos. This scam also failed and she was sentenced to seven years in prison for theft.

The Two of Pentacles symbolises fun and recreation but it can also represent obstacles and agitation, although these will be more imagined than real. This card could mean there are two choices that have to be decided upon, and the reader will have to select one or the other in the future.

Ann Debar earned a living by spinning outlandish stories and playing on people's imaginations. She had many opportunities to choose a legitimate path, but still persisted in her frauds after she no longer needed to.

Three of Pentacles

Christoph Haizmann

Christoph was a painter who performed a ritual invocation to summon the devil in 1666. He had been severely depressed following the death of his father, so he asked the devil to become his father figure. After the invocation Christoph moved to Austria and found minor success with his painting career. His pact with the devil required him to surrender his soul in 1677, and he sought out a priest to perform an exorcism to help him break the pact. The exorcism was carried out in two sessions at a cathedral in Mariazell, Austria. Afterward, Christoph retired to a monastery. He painted a series of illustrations showing his encounters with the devil, but the originals were lost and only the copies remain.

> The Three of Pentacles indicates artistic ability and skilled labour. It can also mean fame and recognition for a person's work. Christoph Haizmann never requested success or fame from the devil; he only wished to have his depression relieved. Once this had been accomplished he was able to use his natural artistic abilities to prosper and earn a living. The Three of Pentacles may be suggesting the reader should utilise their artistic gifts.

Four of Pentacles
Cixi

Cixi was born into a Manchu noble family and became a concubine of the Chinese emperor at the age of 16. She gave birth to his only child, who in turn became the emperor. Cixi was appointed as regent, a position she used to rule China for 47 years. As empress dowager Cixi consolidated power for herself and kept the young emperor in a state of subservience to her. When he died from stress and disease his successor was also controlled by Cixi, who permitted no one to question her authority.

She was a conservative woman who distrusted Western science and new technologies. She diverted funds intended to modernise China's navy to the construction of her summer palace. During the Boxer Rebellion, Cixi made it legal to murder any foreigner on Chinese soil. Before dying in 1908 she poisoned the emperor to ensure he couldn't reverse any of her policies. However, she left China in a weakened state and it was soon torn apart by civil war.

The Four of Pentacles indicates inheritance, legacy and greed for material possessions. The pentacles on this card are woven into Cixi's dress, where they cannot be easily removed. She never relinquished her power and her descendants inherited a broken country unable to move into the modern era.

Five of Pentacles
Donner Party

The Donner Party was a group of 87 pioneers who set off from Independence, Missouri in May 1846, travelling to California in search of a better life. The journey was organised by George Donner and James Reed. Travel along the Oregon Trail in the 1800s was extremely dangerous, and the party had a series of mishaps that slowed their journey and drained their supplies. When they arrived far behind schedule in the Sierra Nevada Mountains they wound up stuck in a snowstorm and had to spend winter on the mountain.

When the food ran out the Donner Party began to starve, and before long they started eating their dead friends and family out of necessity. Tensions between the families led to multiple murders, and those slain bodies were also eaten. Of the 87 people who first set out, 42 died without reaching California.

The Five of Pentacles is a card that indicates want, privation and destitution. The image of the Donner Party on this card contains no pentacles, to symbolise their lack of material sustenance. The hardship they faced was partly bad luck and partly poor decision-making. Seeing this card in a reading may be a warning to carefully choose your next step.

Six of Pentacles
Weyn Ockers

Weyn came from a wealthy Protestant family in Amsterdam. She became involved in the iconoclastic riots against the Catholic Church, a movement that sought to eliminate the veneration of sacred statues. At the Oude Kerk in Amsterdam a priest named Simon Alewijnsz erected a status of the Virgin Mary and told girls to leave money and valuables as tokens of honour at the altar. The money was used to pay the legal fees of a priest who had been jailed for persecuting Dutch Protestants.

When the iconoclastic riots began, Weyn joined the angry mob and started destroying statues all around the city. She entered the Oude Kerk and threw her slipper at the statue of the Virgin Mary, shattering the glass case around it and breaking its foot. For this she was arrested and found guilty of heresy, and she was subsequently drowned inside a wine barrel in the town square in 1568.

> The Six of Pentacles represents gifts and giving and can also indicate a need for attention or vigilance. Weyn detested the way religious statues were used to collect money from the faithful and gave her life in trying to bring an end to the practice.

Seven of Pentacles
La Quintrala

Catalina de los Ríos was the daughter of a prosperous landowner in Santiago, Chile. Due to her red hair and fiery temperament she was nicknamed 'La Quintrala' after a red Chilean flower. In 1650 she became the master of a large estate and actively managed the business. She mercilessly whipped her slaves for minor offences or because they glared at her in a certain way. Her bloodlust escalated and she began murdering her slaves and the tenant farmers who worked her land. She was arrested on charges of murder, but her political connections and money resulted in the charges being dropped. Just prior to her death at the age of 61 she made a full confession of her sins and left most of her estate to the Catholic Church as penance for her crimes.

The Seven of Pentacles represents business and bartering. It can also indicate arguments. This card indicates positive business arrangements and an enterprise that will be successful. La Quintrala is shown whipping her servants while they work, playing on the sometimes quarrelsome nature of this card, and the golden fields can be expected to yield riches in the future.

Eight of Pentacles
William de Soules

William II de Soules, Lord of Liddesdale and known as Bad Lord Soules, came from an ancient and respected noble Scottish family. He fought alongside Robert the Bruce during the border wars for Scottish independence. Lord Soules was a necromancer and sorcerer who summoned a familiar spirit named Robin Redcap out of a locked chest. The chronicles say he made a pact with the devil whereby he would grow rich and have success while the devil would receive the souls of the people Soules killed. From his stronghold at Hermitage Castle, Lord Soules terrorised the peasants working his land.

After being convicted of trying to murder the king he escaped from prison, but his former tenants captured him and boiled him alive in a cauldron of oil at a stone circle called Ninestane Rig.

The Eight of Pentacles represents work or employment and also craftsmanship or a particular skill that can be used to earn money. There is a certain amount of ambition present as well. The card depicts Bad Lord Soules in his castle with Robin Redcap dancing on a chest. The pentacles of wealth and power are hidden inside and can only be accessed through practising the dark art of necromancy.

Nine of Pentacles

Don Pedro Jaramillo

Pedro Jaramillo was born in Guadalajara, Mexico in 1829 to indigenous parents. He settled in Los Olmos Ranch, Texas and began working as a *curandero*, a traditional faith healer. Pedro's reputation for kindness and generosity grew as quickly as his reputation for healing. He had a standard policy of only charging 50 cents or a dollar for his cures, and if someone could not pay he performed the cure anyway. Some people donated much more out of gratitude for being healed.

When he died on 3 July 1907 it was a great loss to the community. At the place of his old residence a shrine was built with a life-sized bust of the great curandero to preserve his memory. Thousands of people go every year to pay their respects and ask Don Pedro for healing.

The Nine of Pentacles indicates safety and success. General well-being and goodness of heart will be present. Don Pedro is depicted in the act of healing, and there are nine coins scattered on the ground. He not only used his natural talents to help others but received more wealth than he could spend in a lifetime.

Ten of Pentacles

Helen Duncan

Helen was a Scottish trance medium who was able to materialise ectoplasm during her séances. In 1944 she was the last person tried under the 1735 Witchcraft Act. With the aid of her husband Henry, Helen performed séances for audiences all over Great Britain. She became a darling of the spiritualist community, which fervently believed in her abilities to communicate with the spirits of the dead.

One of Helen's key attractions involved making ectoplasm appear out of thin air. Further investigation revealed this was simple cheesecloth that had been swallowed then regurgitated during the séance. She was arrested for fraud on two occasions and spent nine months in prison. Despite this she remained a popular medium until her death in 1956.

The Ten of Pentacles represents riches and financial gain. These may be connected with the home or otherwise tied to family matters. Helen Duncan conjured an entire career out of thin air through her talent of swallowing cheesecloth. The card depicts coins falling from her nose as though they are ghostly riches.

Page of Pentacles

Samuel Liddell MacGregor Mathers

Mathers was a ritual magician and author who founded the Hermetic Order of the Golden Dawn, a magical fraternity, at the turn of the century. Mathers joined the Masons in 1877 and befriended British occultist Kenneth Mackenzie, who introduced him to ritual magic. He left the Masons to focus on studying the Kabbalah and finding practical uses for its rituals.

Mathers translated and published many old occult manuscripts, including *The Kabbalah Unveiled*. Although he never sought publicity or fame his involvement with other occultists of the time, including Aleister Crowley, caused tremendous friction in the Golden Dawn and he eventually left to start his own temple, Alpha et Omega.

The Page of Pentacles represents study, scholarship and reflection and can also indicate a person who is delivering a message. The card depicts Samuel Mathers in the act of performing a ritual. The chequered pattern on the floor indicates he is in a Golden Dawn temple. His costume was designed for the rites of Isis, and his success is evident by the astral pentacle that has appeared above him. The message inherent is one of financial rewards and future success.

Knight of Pentacles
Phalaris

Phalaris, who was known as the Tyrant of Akragas, was the ruler of southern Sicily from 570 to 554 BCE. Under his rule the city became extremely prosperous, but his cruelty toward his subjects was legendary. The tyrant eventually made himself lord of the entire island of Sicily, although as he became increasingly successful he also grew more malicious in his punishments toward anyone who defied him.

In 544 BCE the citizens of Sicily rose up and overthrew Phalaris. They utilised his favourite torture device, a giant sculpture of a bull fashioned entirely from brass. He was placed inside this monstrous device and a fire was lit underneath. As the brass heated up the tyrant was slowly cooked alive by the hot metal.

The Knight of Pentacles represents someone who is useful and has skills that will be of service. It may indicate an inheritance or money from an unexpected source. The card shows Phalaris inside the brazen bull being roasted alive, while the coins of his treasury lie scattered before him. He was a clever administrator who made his country rich, but once he had outlived his usefulness he was destroyed in his own creation.

Queen of Pentacles

Catharina de Chasseur

Born in France in 1490, Catharina married a Dutch nobleman and moved to The Hague. She later became involved in a counterfeiting scheme and was sentenced to death. Catharina married into the highly influential municipality of Assendelft in The Netherlands as a teenager, but from the beginning her husband regretted his decision to marry her. As a common girl she was scorned and treated poorly by the entire family, and she eventually moved out of their palace and was given an allowance.

When Catharina's husband learned that men had been visiting her home he cut off the allowance, forcing her to find other means of support. Although she had established a profitable merchant business she began a counterfeiting operation in the basement of her house that minted fake coins. She was caught and executed by being drowned with water poured directly down her throat until she choked. After her death the Assendelft mansion appeared to be haunted for many years, with water mysteriously pouring from the dining room ceiling.

The Queen of Pentacles represents magnificence, financial security and opulence. In this context the image of Catharina on the card needs no explanation: she is surrounded by coins and reads quietly, entirely sure of her position.

King of Pentacles
Ratu Udre Udre

Udre Udre was known as the Cannibal King of Fiji, and is recognised by the *Guinness World Records* as the most prolific cannibal. His total, recognised victim count is stated to be between 872 and 999 people.

From the time Udre Udre was young he only ate human flesh occasionally, as was the common practice of his tribe. As he grew older and his power among his people increased he began eating more and more of his enemies. After Udre Udre became chief of his people he wasn't content to sit on the throne. In 1840, when his power was at its peak, he was suddenly executed by the combined efforts of the British and the king of Bau. Today, the locals who live near the site of his old village refuse to visit the site alone out of fear of Udre Udre's spirit.

The King of Pentacles indicates business and intellectual aptitude, including mathematical ability. There is some pride represented on this card, but also protection. Udre Udre only ate his vanquished enemies, never his own people. He is depicted sitting calmly atop a pile of human skulls, showing that his high position came through his skilful conquest of those who opposed him.

Ace of Swords
Raynald of Châtillon

Raynald was a French crusader who gained a reputation for repeatedly violating treaties between the Christian and Muslim leaders, making enemies among both factions. He started his career in the Crusades fighting as a mercenary for King Baldwin III of Jerusalem and became the prince of Antioch (modern-day Syria) by marrying Princess Constance. As ruler of Antioch, Raynald invaded and sacked the Byzantine territory of Cyprus, subjecting the island to a three-week orgy of violence.

While raiding Muslim caravans for plunder Raynald was captured and imprisoned for 15 years. Upon his release he married Lady Oultrejordain and took up residence in Kerak Castle. He spent a few more years killing innocent Muslim pilgrims before his ignominious defeat at the Battle of Hattin in 1187. After the battle he was executed by the Muslim sultan Saladin for refusing to convert to Islam.

The Ace of Swords is connected with the element of air and represents conquest and triumph by force. It may signal either great prosperity or great misery. When looking at the image on the card you can see the airy influence but may wonder if Raynald is the knight or the head on the tip of the sword.

Two of Swords

Thomas More

Thomas More was a prolific writer of books on religion, government and law as well as poetry. He became a fervent Catholic during his years as a student, which brought him into conflict with Henry VIII.

More's work as a government administrator led to his favour with King Henry VIII, who selected him in 1529 as lord chancellor after Cardinal Wolsey's dismissal. At the time Henry was in the process of breaking England away from the Catholic Church, which caused a terrible rift between More and the king. More was dismissed and later brought to trial on charges of treason for statements he made against the pope's supremacy over the king. He was beheaded and his head placed on a pike on London Bridge. Because he died for his devotion, Sir Thomas More was canonised as a saint by the Catholic Church.

The Two of Swords represents friendship and courage. Thomas More, depicted on the card after his execution, died due to his friendship with Henry VIII and his courageous refusal to back down from his faith. Friendship sometimes requires us to be blind to the actions of our friends, a lesson More would have been wise to learn.

Three of Swords
Ivan the Terrible

Ivan IV Vasilyevich was declared tsar of Russia in 1547 at the age of 16, following in the footsteps of his father, who had been grand prince of Moscow. His reputation was damaged by fits of mental instability. Throughout his reign as tsar Ivan engaged in constant warfare, and was responsible for expanding Russia's territory with a campaign into Siberia. He was married at least six times and had eight children. Ivan's Orthodox faith was based firmly on his belief in his right to rule as God's instrument on earth.

Ivan murdered his eldest son after a period of tension between them that culminated in Ivan kicking his pregnant daughter-in-law and causing her to miscarry. During the subsequent argument they became physical and Ivan stabbed his son to death. Afterward, he cried: 'May I be damned, I've killed my son!'

> The Three of Swords indicates absence, removal, oppression and worry and can foretell of bad news. Much of the pain in the card is not physical, but rather mental strain and troubles of the heart. When Ivan killed his favourite son in a fit of rage his heart was broken as he had forever lost what he loved.

Four of Swords

Johannes Kelpius

Johannes was a Lutheran mystic from Romania who founded a religious sect in a cave in Philadelphia, Pennsylvania in the late 1600s. A student of music, botany, theology and astronomy, his belief that the end of the world would occur in 1694 was based on numerological interpretations of Revelations 12: 6: 'And the woman fled into the wilderness, where she hath a place prepared of God, that they should feed her there a thousand two hundred and threescore days.'

Johannes and his followers lived in caves and strived to form a communal utopia. He preached the virtues of simplicity, celibacy and peace and taught his followers the secrets of numerology, astrology and other occult subjects. Some say he discovered the philosopher's stone, only to throw it into the river before his death.

The Four of Swords represents solitude and repose. It can indicate a period of inactivity or rest but may also suggest the passing away of a person or their influence. This card shows Johannes Kelpius in prayerful meditation inside his cave. Four swords have been cast off, which is emblematic of his devotion to peace.

Five of Swords
François l'Olonnais

François l'Olonnais was a French pirate who was active throughout the Caribbean from 1660 to 1668 whose primary targets were Spanish ships travelling to the New World. François had a vendetta against the Spanish that stemmed from an incident in which his men were attacked while shipwrecked in Mexico. François had been forced to play dead by smearing himself with blood and hiding under the bodies of his crew.

His most glorious feat came from the sack of the San Carlos de la Barra Fortress on the Maracaibo coast of Venezuela. His men raped and pillaged the entire coastline before torturing and murdering the garrison in the fort. During a scouting expedition in Panama, François was ambushed by the Kuna Indians and torn to pieces while still alive.

The Five of Swords indicates destruction, dishonour and loss. It may also indicate feelings of bitterness toward the world. This card does not have to mean an absolute defeat but may be simply a loss from which the reader will recover. François is depicted in a fierce battle with the Kuna warriors and has let slip his sword. Although some of his attackers have been wounded, he will not win the battle.

Six of Swords

RMS *Titanic*

The Royal Mail Ship *Titanic* was a British passenger liner operated by the White Star Line that sank in the ocean on 15 April 1912 after hitting an iceberg during her maiden voyage. At the time she was launched *Titanic* was the largest passenger ship that had ever been built and was advertised as being unsinkable. In the middle of the freezing North Atlantic Ocean, the ship hit an iceberg and began taking on water. There were not enough lifeboats to safely evacuate everyone from the ship, which resulted in 1,514 dead with only 710 survivors.

The sinking of the *Titanic* was a massive tragedy that continues to resonate. Many famous and wealthy members of high society were on board and went down with the ship, perishing in the icy waters.

The Six of Swords indicates a journey by water and also journeys in general. If a trip is already scheduled this card suggests it will be a pleasant one. It has much to do with the conceptual idea of a road ahead or a path that has already been taken. The card shows the massive ocean liner sailing past icebergs that, combined with its smokestacks, form the impression of swords sealing its fate.

Seven of Swords

Darya Nikolayevna Saltykova

SEVEN OF SWORDS

Darya Nikolayevna Saltykova

Darya Ivanova was born into a Russian noble family in 1730. Six months after her husband Gleb, a soldier, died she became increasingly unbalanced and began abusing the serfs who worked on her estate. Her favourite targets were beautiful young women: when attacking them she loved pulling their hair until their scalp bled, often ripping the hair out by the roots. If a serf caught Darya when she was feeling particularly cruel they could expect to be tortured with boiling water or have their hair burned off right down to the scalp.

Two serfs finally ran away and filed a complaint with the empress Catherine the Great. Darya was arrested, tried and sentenced to life imprisonment. Her prison cell was in the basement and she could be viewed by peasants on the street, who brought their children and treated her like a freak.

The Seven of Swords represents a plan that will be attempted but is likely to fail. It may also indicate an argument or the ability to influence someone else with words. Darya is pictured stabbing her victim, an act she believes she cannot be punished for. She doesn't realise the new empress will not tolerate the murder of serfs and she will suffer in the future for her actions.

Eight of Swords

Lilias Adie

During the night of 28 July 1704 in Torryburn, a small village about 16 kilometres north-west of Edinburgh, Lilias Adie was arrested by the local bailie and incarcerated after being accused of witchcraft by a local woman. Lilias was questioned, and she admitted to making a pact with the devil and serving him with other witches. Her story of meeting the devil and working with him and other witches was as detailed as it was fantastic, but her judges ate it up.

In reality Lilias knew she would fare better if she told long stories that implicated no one else by name. She did not want to be tortured, and confessing was the only way to make sure that wouldn't happen. The only names she provided were of people who had been executed during previous witch trials, thereby protecting other innocent people from being arrested. She died in prison due to her age and the harsh conditions.

The Eight of Swords indicates bad news, a crisis, conflict or illness. There will be obstacles that must be overcome, and the reader may not have the skills required to do so on their own. Lilias restrained in prison is symbolic of her inability to escape from the challenge she is facing.

Nine of Swords
Livonian Werewolf

Old Thiess was an 80-year-old man who was arrested in Livonia on suspicion of committing witchcraft. During his trial he openly admitted to transforming into a werewolf and roaming the countryside. Thiess claimed to be a werewolf in the service of God who only killed servants of the devil. He seemed to have perpetual good health, and aside from his unusual claims he appeared to possess otherwise perfect mental clarity. The judges did not believe his story and dismissed the trial. Afterward, his reputation as a werewolf spread and people from all around Livonia came to him for healing, blessings and magical charms.

Thiess was brought to the court again and told to stop performing faith healings. He tried to back out from his previous statements but admitted he had never been to church and didn't believe most of the tenants of Christianity. The judges ordered him to be flogged and exiled, a punishment that likely caused his death.

The Nine of Swords represents death, failure, disappointment and despair. It may also suggest intolerance or sorrow. Poor Old Thiess only wished to do good, but his naive worldview was his undoing. This card may also indicate serious challenges in the future and could be a warning to prepare yourself for the worst rather than naively pretending everything will be all right.

Ten of Swords

Bridget Bishop

Bridget Bishop was the first person during the Salem witch trials to be executed for practising witchcraft. Her death ushered in a wave of further executions that resulted in the deaths of 25 accused witches. On 18 April 1692 Bridget was accused of bewitching five young women, and a warrant for her apprehension was issued the same day along with warrants for three others also accused of witchcraft. Bridget and the others were victims of the witchcraft panic then enveloping Salem.

Bridget's response was simple: 'I am innocent. I know nothing of it. I have done no witchcraft.' To each subsequent accusation she made a similar statement of innocence and ignorance, often denying having ever met or seen her accuser. She was convicted of leading an immoral life and practising witchcraft and was sentenced to death by hanging.

The Ten of Swords indicates pain, affliction and sadness and may also suggest treason or betrayal. The card depicts Bridget Bishop being hung, with the swords of her accusers pointing toward her. The airy nature of the suit of Swords is evidenced in her hanging, and as the wind blows her legacy will be transformed from that of a criminal to that of a martyr.

Page of Swords
Chief Leatherlips

Chief Leatherlips was an important chief of the Wyandot nation who advocated peaceful cooperation with the United States as it expanded further westward into native territory. His Wyandot name was Sha-Te-Yah-Ron-Aa, but on account of the chief's honest dealings and his reputation for never breaking his word the white settlers called him 'Leatherlips'.

In early 1810 Chief Tecumseh sent a delegation to persuade Leatherlips to turn against the Americans and join his confederation of Indian nations. Leatherlips refused, and consequently Tecumseh's brother accused him of bewitching the delegation and demanded he be put to death. Leatherlips didn't fight his accusers but did accept their judgement, and he was executed with a tomahawk. Afterward Tecumseh was defeated at the disastrous Battle of Tippecanoe, while Leatherlips was celebrated as a martyred hero.

The Page of Swords represents authority, management and someone who approaches a problem from an intellectual angle. It can also indicate spying or intense examination.

Knight of Swords
Vseslav of Polotsk

KNIGHT OF SWORDS

Vseslav of Polotsk

Vseslav was the ruler of a principality located in northern Belarus. Due to his proficiency in battle he took on a legendary status as a werewolf who ran through the night to attack his target with great speed. During the siege of Novgorod it was rumoured that by night, while the army was resting, he used his magic to become a falcon and observe the enemy from above. The soldiers of the Kievan Rus developed a saying: 'The retinue sleeps, but the magician sleeps not.'

Vseslav conquered the city of Kiev and was crowned its grand prince. Russian folk hero Il'ja Muromec was warned while marching to liberate Kiev: 'Do not march against Vseslav the magician. If he does not take you by force, he will use cleverness and wisdom.'

The Knight of Swords represents skill and bravery and may also indicate war, destruction, opposition and resistance. Just like Vseslav there is fast movement in the card, cutting through the air as the blade of a sword does. Whatever comes will come quickly. There may be an element of revenge or of a past wrong being made right.

Queen of Swords
Lizzie Borden

Lizzie Borden was tried and acquitted of murdering her parents with an axe in the city of Fall River, Massachusetts in 1892. Although found innocent, most of the evidence pointed to her guilt. Lizzie waited in the upstairs bedroom with a small hatchet and attacked her stepmother Abby, delivering more than 17 whacks to Abby's face. When her father arrived home Lizzie fell upon him in the living room, hacking at him 11 times and leaving his bloody corpse on the couch.

During the investigation many other suspects were considered, although none as seriously as Lizzie. She claimed to have been sitting in the hayloft of the barn eating pears while the murders were occurring. With the inheritance she received Lizzie bought a house outside of town and lived there without further notoriety until she died of pneumonia in 1927 at the age of 66.

The Queen of Swords indicates female sadness and embarrassment and may also signify mourning or loss. There is little in the woman depicted on the card that may be considered charming, and she will be stern and possibly overbearing. Like Lizzie she wields the weapons at her disposal with keen ability.

King of Swords
Richard III

Richard, briefly the Duke of Gloucester, became the king of England after he murdered several members of his family to clear a path to assume the throne. He began his military training at the age of 14 and commanded troops on behalf of his brother, King Edward IV. His physical proportions were short and slight and one shoulder was higher than the other, a condition caused by scoliosis that grew more pronounced as he aged.

Richard arranged for his brother, the Duke of Clarence, to be imprisoned and executed on charges of treason and witchcraft. After Edward IV died he had his nephews murdered and was proclaimed king in 1483. He didn't reign long enough to have a significant impact on national affairs and was killed in battle against Henry Tudor, the future King Henry VII.

The King of Swords represents power, authority, judgement and the law. Unlike in the traditional tarot, Richard's sword is pointed downward toward the earth. He was a soldier but was unable to win a war for his own kingdom. His talents for manipulating the law and his family members ended up being his true strength.

Ace of Wands
Roger Bolingbroke

Roger Bolingbroke was an astrologer who was renowned in London in the 1440s for the accuracy of his predictions. In late 1440 Bolingbroke was asked by Duchess Eleanor of Gloucester to cast a horoscope predicting King Henry VI's future; at the time a horoscope cast for the king could be considered treason if it revealed a bad omen.

The horoscope he created for the king indicated that an accident would occur that would cause the king's death, and that as a result of the death Eleanor's husband would ascend to the throne. The king's council learned of the horoscope and arrested Bolingbroke on charges of necromancy and treason. He was hanged, drawn and quartered. Before his death he admitted going 'too far in my cunning'.

The Ace of Wands represents creation and the starting point of an enterprise. There is an effect of suddenness inherent in this card, which depicts Bolingbroke using his powers to summon a demon spirit. The act of creation and the fire of imagination are closely tied to the suit of Wands and the ace in particular.

Two of Wands

Antoine Court de Gébelin

Antoine was a prolific author born in 1719 who wrote an early text about the tarot. Although it was not his primary interest, his treatise formed the foundation of modern interpretations of tarot card meanings. He attended a theological seminary in Switzerland and studied to be a Protestant minister like his father. After teaching for a few years he moved to Paris and devoted himself to the acquisition and propagation of knowledge about literature, science and the arts.

Antoine's greatest achievement is an exhaustive, encyclopaedic book about the history of civilisation titled *Le Monde primitif* that was printed in an astounding 11 volumes. One chapter tells a story of the tarot, explaining it originated in Egypt in a book that 'escaped the flames that devoured their superb library' and made its way to Europe disguised in the artwork of the tarot. However, the story Antoine tells is entirely untrue and he provides no sources to substantiate his claims.

The Two of Wands represents riches, fortune and magnificence, but also sadness and suffering. It may indicate economic or creative projects such as Antoine's massive book about human history.

Three of Wands
Saint Guinefort

Saint Guinefort was a greyhound dog who lived during the 1100s in central France. Although not officially recognised by the Catholic Church, Guinefort was revered by peasants in the Lyon region who celebrated the dog as a protector of children. The dog was owned by a knight and was left alone with the knight's child one day. A snake entered the nursery and Guinefort attacked it, saving the child's life. When the knight entered he saw the dog covered with blood and assumed he had hurt the child. Without thinking he killed Guinefort.

Once the truth was discovered the knight fell into a deep depression. The castle was destroyed shortly after and the estate turned into a wasteland. Locals planted a tree on the dog's grave, believing he could save their children from sickness or injury. They continued their worship of Guinefort as a folk saint until Father Stephen of Bourbon cut down the tree and burned the dog's bones.

The Three of Wands indicates a cooperative endeavour that will be beneficial. It may also suggest commerce, strength in all its forms and the discovery of new ideas.

Four of Wands
Nicholas II

Nicholas II was the last tsar of all the Russias before being deposed by Communist revolutionaries led by Vladimir Lenin. Despite his training, when the time came for his coronation after the death of his father Nicholas remarked, 'I am not yet ready to be tsar. I know nothing of the business of ruling.' However, after his coronation in 1896 he was assured that God had ordained his rule and nobody could dispute his divine right.

Within 20 years of his coronation Nicholas's disastrous policies led to the steep decline of Russian military prestige and economic power. The Soviets seized control of the country and arrested Nicholas and his family. In July 1918 they were all executed in the basement of a remote house, although they were later declared saints in the Russian Orthodox Church.

The Four of Wands represents family circumstances and home life. One aspect in Tsar Nicholas's life in which he didn't fail was in his loyalty to his family: he cared for them and made certain they were comfortable right until the end. The four bayonets of Soviet rifles pointing toward the imperial family replace the four walls of their happy home.

Five of Wands

Jan Hus

Jan Hus was a minister who preached against the excesses of the Catholic Church. He was responsible for setting the stage for later reformers such as Martin Luther and John Calvin.

Inspired by the philosophy of Oxford theologian John Wycliffe, Jan began to preach that the head of the church was Jesus Christ and not the pope. As rage toward Catholic practices spread across Bohemia, the pope's anger grew stronger and he issued an edict condemning Jan and his version of the gospel. Jan was arrested and tried for heresy. At his trial he asked for his doctrinal statements to be read, and if anyone was willing to argue against them to produce scriptural evidence of why Jan's statements were wrong. Then he would recant. The judges viewed this as a confession and he was burned at the stake in 1415.

The Five of Wands indicates a struggle for riches and gain, which may include elements of theatre and could even indicate a performance battle instead of a real one. After his death Jan's supporters revolted against the pope and launched the Hussite Wars. This conflict was little more than one Christian fighting against another for supremacy of their preferred religious doctrine, much like the mock warfare indicated on this card.

Six of Wands

Nostradamus

Michel de Nostradame is almost as famous today as he was during his lifetime, from 1503 to 1566. A French astrologer, his wisdom and vision were such that his writings are still consulted today and held up as portents of future events.

Nostradamus developed a treatment for the plague in the form of a rose pill, which brought him some financial security. However, his wife and children died from the plague, which left him devastated. After these losses he began to meditate, and he locked himself away and sought visions of the future in bowls filled with water and herbs. He wrote his first almanac in 1550, and it was successful enough for him to keep writing them. He amassed a work of more than 6,000 prophecies. His most famous book, Le Prophéties, was a collection of his prophecies written in quatrains and cryptic code to avoid charges of heresy.

The Six of Wands indicates a message or a messenger bringing good news. There is also a suggestion of special abilities or insight. Nostradamus is pictured in the act of writing with a fresh stylus, while five more sit idle on his desk. He is preparing to bring messages of good fortune for the world to read with his unique gift of prophecy.

Seven of Wands

Charles Lwanga

Charles Lwanga was leader of the Ugandan Martyrs, a group of Christians who were executed for refusing to accept the authority of the king of Buganda. In 1885 Charles became master of the pages to King Mwanga II. At this time it was common practice for the king to use his young male pages as sexual playthings. Charles had recently converted to Christianity and convinced many of the pages to do the same, and as a result they began to refuse to submit to the king's lustful urges.

Mwanga viewed the boys' refusal to have sex with him as a challenge to his authority as king. He commanded Charles to stop preaching the gospel to them and to arrange sexual liaisons. Charles refused, saying he would rather serve God than serve the king, and he and the other pages who had converted to Christianity were burned alive. As Charles burned he said, 'Poor madman, you are burning me, but it is as if you are pouring water on my body.'

The Seven of Wands indicates valour and success in a conflict. It can also stand for negotiations and competition, especially in business.

Eight of Wands
Saint Sebastian

Saint Sebastian was a Roman officer who was executed for converting to Christianity. The image of his execution became a popular subject for artists wishing to depict the male body and holy suffering. Sebastian rose to become a member of the Praetorian Guard but worked to secretly convert Roman citizens to Christianity. When Diocletian discovered his activities, Sebastian was sentenced to death.

The executioners stripped him naked and tied him to a tree then they fired a hail of arrows into him, but none of the shots pierced his major organs. Although injured, he survived the attack and was nursed back to health. When the emperor discovered Sebastian was still alive he had him arrested and beaten to death. His body was buried in the location of the future Basilica of Saint Sebastian in Rome.

The Eight of Wands indicates activity in undertakings, an express message and the speed of events in general. The arrows flying through Saint Sebastian are arrows of passion: his passion for religion and the passion his image provokes in others.

Nine of Wands

Urbain Grandier

Urbain Grandier was a French priest who was accused of making a pact with the devil in the early 1600s. He was burned at the stake for 'magic, maleficence, and possession'. Success as a preacher brought Grandier temptations he could not resist, and he developed a reputation for sleeping with local married women. He was arrested and tried for adultery but not convicted. In 1632 the nuns of a local convent began to suffer from sickness. A doctor failed to determine the cause, and rumours spread that it was the result of demonic possession.

During an attempted exorcism the nuns accused Urbain Grandier of bewitching them. He was questioned, but defiantly dismissed the accusations. His case was brought before the Crown prosecutor, who presented Grandier's occult manuscripts and a pact signed in blood between the priest and several demons. This was all they needed to convict and execute him.

> The Nine of Wands represents an attack, but one that is met with bold action. Even though the opposition is strong it will be overcome. This card can also indicate adversity, delay and trouble.

Ten of Wands
Margaret Aitken

Margaret Aitken was an accused Scottish witch who became a witch finder in the service of the government. When she was arrested on suspicion of being a witch she avoided torture by quickly confessing that she had participated in many rituals to summon the devil and had made a pact with Satan. She said she had the ability to identify a witch by peering into their eyes. The witch hunters took her seriously and began touring Scotland, putting her powers to work. Hundreds of innocent people were put to death based solely on Margaret's testimony.

In Glasgow, she was exposed as a fraud and was burned at the stake. Her ruse proved an embarrassment to King James VI, and he suspended further witch hunts for the rest of his reign.

The Ten of Wands is a card that usually represents oppression and difficulties; however, it can also indicate fortune and success that will come after passing through those challenges. There is some fear and cowardice in the card, like Margaret's fear at being tortured, which led her to needlessly condemn others to death simply to save herself. She did not go to the flames with an honourable heart but was instead screaming in terror.

Page of Wands

Mervyn Tuchet

Mervyn Tuchet was born in 1593 into a minor noble family in south-western England. After inheriting his father's estate and wealth and becoming the 2nd Earl of Castlehaven he became a depraved madman who engaged in sexual excesses of all kinds.

The earl hired numerous young Irishmen as members of his household and routinely had sex with all of them in front of his wife and other servants. He often forced his wife and stepdaughter to also submit to having sex with the household members. Mervyn once hosted a two-week orgy with a prostitute who ended up giving everyone in the house syphilis. After this his wife and son reported his conduct to King Charles I and Mervyn was arrested on charges of sodomy and rape. During the trial many scandalous details were revealed, and he was sentenced to death.

The Page of Wands signifies a dark young man who is a lover or may be in search of a woman. It may also suggest the presence of a rival lover. In any case, the card indicates someone who is searching for something. Mervyn was a libertine who was constantly looking for the next pleasurable experience to satisfy his lust, which proved to be bottomless.

Knight of Wands

Joan of Arc

The Maid of Orleans was a French peasant girl who began having holy visions that inspired her to join the cause of Dauphine Charles against English invaders. She arrived at Orleans fortress while it was under siege. Carrying a banner embroidered with holy symbols and riding a white horse, she inspired the French soldiers and they won the battle. With her help the dauphine was crowned as the king of France.

However, once the English asked for peace Joan became a liability to France and was turned over to Bishop Pierre Cauchon. The bishop tried her for heresy for claiming she had spoken to God and also for wearing men's clothes. Before being executed Joan was asked if she enjoyed killing English soldiers, and she replied, 'I loved my banner ten times better than I loved my sword.' She requested that it be held where she could see it while being burned alive.

The Knight of Wands is on a journey, searching for something lost in the unknown. Exploration and travel are indicated. As depicted on the card Joan wears armour and carries a sword but both of her hands are firmly on her banner, which indicates her goal is spiritual rather than militant.

Queen of Wands
Marie Anne Lenormand

Marie Lenormand was a fortune-teller who specialised in cartomancy, which is telling the future through the use of a pack of playing cards. During the French Revolution Marie opened a bookshop in Paris, where she told fortunes for members of the upper class who were in desperate fear for their lives. She became rich and successful by offering people a glimmer of hope for their future.

Marie was arrested during the Reign of Terror for associating with aristocrats, but this proved to be a blessing when she met the future empress Josephine in prison. Marie became a friend and close adviser to Josephine and followed her into Napoleon's imperial court. After her death in 1843 at the age of 71 her estate was given to her nephew, who accepted the money but burned her occult items.

The Queen of Wands is a woman who is friendly, helpful, loving and honourable. It is a card that symbolises good business and a desire for money. Marie Lenormand is pictured holding a wand and cards, the tools she used to conjure an excellent life for herself.

King of Wands

Vlad Dracula

Vlad Dracula, commonly known as Vlad the Impaler, was the ruler of Wallachia on three separate occasions and gained a reputation for using excessive violence and psychological warfare to defeat his enemies.

As a child in the mediaeval town of Sighişoara, Vlad watched many criminal executions, which may have sparked his love of violence. With the aid of the Ottoman Empire he came to power in Wallachia, but was betrayed by them and forced to ask Hungary for help. When the Ottomans invaded Vlad waged a guerrilla campaign, attacking the larger force in daring night raids. He prevented their conquest of the country by staging the Forest of the Impaled, a massive line of bodies impaled on stakes. This drove the invaders back, but Vlad was eventually captured. He later died in battle and his head was displayed in Istanbul.

The King of Wands represents a dark man who is honest and provides material and emotional security to the reader. He is austere and intellectual, like Vlad the Impaler, finding creative solutions to difficult problems. This card might indicate a creative pursuit or forthcoming news involving business.

About the author

Travis McHenry is the author of *Occult Tarot*, *Angel Tarot* and *Vlad Dracula Tarot*. He studied anthropology at Bloomsburg University of Pennsylvania and is a practising occultist and ritual magician.

Travis was first introduced to magic while researching a coven of witches in rural Pennsylvania known as the Coven of the Catta. His experiences with the coven led him to write the first biography of their leader, Dr Frederick Santee, which became his inspiration to create the *Magicians, Martyrs, and Madmen Tarot*.

travismchenry.com
travis.mchenry
bloodstone.tarot

About the illustrator

 ristin Gottberg is a Venezuelan artist with a passion for digital design. She has had almost a decade of experience illustrating everything from children's books to government publications.

Notes